Sharyn McCrumb's Appalachia

A Collection of Essays on the Mountain South

To Libby—
Best wishes—

Sharyn McCrumb

Sharyn McCrumb
Oct 8, 2011
Decatur

Sharyn McCrumb's Appalachia. Copyright 2011 Sharyn McCrumb. All rights reserved. Printed in the United States of America.

www.oconeespirit.com

Library of Congress Cataloging-in-Publication Data
McCrumb, Sharyn.
Sharyn McCrumb's Appalachia / Sharyn McCrumb

ISBN 978-0-9830040-2-8

1.Mountain life –Appalachian Region, Southern. 2. Appalachian Region, Southern –History. 3.Appalachian Region, Southern –Social life and customs. 4. American literature –Appalachian Region, Southern. 5. Appalachian Region, Southern –Literary collections. 6. Appalachian Region –Literary collections.

Table of Contents

Keepers of the Legends

An essay on the influences of family legends and folklore on fiction

"All around the water tank, standing in the rain,
A thousand miles away from home, waiting for a train..."

When I was four, I thought that was the saddest story in the world. It was a Jimmie Rodgers tune, I later learned, but I only ever heard it sung a cappella by my father in our old Chevrolet on the five-hour drives to visit my grandparents in east Tennessee.

Who was the fellow in the song, I wondered, and how did he get stuck out there on the desolate Texas prairie all alone, so far from the mountains? He seemed to think he was going to make it home all right, but for the duration of the song he was stranded, and I could never hear it without feeling the sting of tears.

I come from a race of storytellers.

My father's family – the Arrowoods and the McCourrys – settled in the Smoky Mountains of western North Carolina in 1790, when the wilderness was still Indian country. They came from the north of England and from Scotland, and they seemed to want mountains, land, and as few neighbors as possible. The first of the McCourrys to settle in America was my great-great-great grandfather Malcolm McCourry, whose story I tell in my novel *The Songcatcher*. Malcolm McCourry was kidnapped as a child from the Scottish island of Islay in the Hebrides in 1750, and made to serve as a crewman on a sailing ship. He later became an attorney in Morristown, New Jersey; fought with the Morris Militia in the American Revolution; and finally settled in what is now Mitchell County, western North Carolina in 1794.

Another (distant) relative, an Arrowood killed in the Battle of Waynesville in May 1865, was the last man to die in the Civil War east of the Mississippi. I recount the search for him in my novel *Ghost Riders*, which won the *Wilma Dykeman Award* for Historical Fiction from the East Tennessee historical Society. *(Through the Honeycutts, I am also a cousin of Wilma Dykeman.)*

Yet another "connection" *(we are cousins-in-law through the Howell family)* is the convicted murderess Frankie Silver, the subject of my 1998 novel, *The Ballad of Frankie Silver.* Frances Stewart Silver (1813-1833) was the first woman hanged for murder in the state of North Carolina. I did not discover the family tie that links us until I began the two years of research prior to writing the novel. I wasn't surprised, though. Since both our families had been in Mitchell County for more than two hundred years, and both produced large numbers of children to intermarry with other families, I knew the connection had to be there. These same bloodlines link both Frankie Silver and me to Appalachian writer Wilma Dykeman *(The French Broad)*, and also to the famous bluegrass musician Del McCoury.

The namesake of my character Spencer Arrowood, my paternal grandfather, worked in the machine shop of the Clinchfield Railroad. He was present on that September day in 1916 at the railroad yard in Erwin, Tennessee when a circus elephant called Mary was hanged for murder: she had killed her trainer in Kingsport. *(I used this last story as a theme in **She Walks These Hills**, in which an elderly escaped convict is the object of a man hunt in the Cherokee National Forest. In the novel the radio disc jockey Hank the Yank reminds his listeners of that story as a prayer for mercy for the hunted fugitive.)*

I grew up listening to my father's tales of World War II in the Pacific, and to older family stories of duels and escapades in Model A Fords. With such adventurers in my background, I grew up seeing the world as a wild and exciting place; the quiet tales of suburban angst so popular in modern fiction are Martian to me.

Two of my great-grandfathers were circuit preachers in the North Carolina mountains a hundred years ago, riding horseback over the ridges to preach in a different community each week. Perhaps they are an indication of our family's regard for books, our gift of storytelling and public-speaking, and our love of the Appalachian mountains, all traits that I acquired as a child.

I have said that my books are like Appalachian quilts. I take brightly colored scraps of legends, ballads, fragments of rural life, and local tragedy, and I piece them together into a complex whole that tells not only a story, but also a deeper truth about the culture of the mountain South.

It is from the family stories, the traditional music, and from my own careful research of the history, folklore, and geography of the region that I gather the squares for these literary quilts.

Storytelling was an art form that I learned early on. When I was a little girl, my father would come in to tell me a bedtime story, which usually began with a phrase like, "Once there was a prince named Paris, whose father was Priam, the king of Troy..." Thus I got the *Iliad* in nightly installments, geared to the level of a four-year old's understanding. I grew up in a swirl of tales: the classics retold; ballads or country songs, each having a melody, but above all a *plot*; and family stories about Civil War soldiers, train wrecks, and lost silver mines.

My mother contributed stories of her father, sixteen-year old John Burdette Taylor, a private in the 68th North Carolina Rangers (CSA), whose regiment walked in rag-bound boots, following the railroad tracks from Virginia to Fort Fisher, site of a decisive North Carolina battle. All his life he would remember leaving footprints of blood in the snow as he marched. When John Taylor returned home to Carteret County in eastern North Carolina at the end of the war, his mother, who was recovering from typhoid, got up out of her sickbed to attend the welcome home party for her son. She died that night.

My father's family fund of Civil War stories involved great-great uncles in western North Carolina who had discovered a silver mine or a valley of ginseng while roaming the hills, trying to escape conscription into one marauding army or the other.

The two sides of the South embodied in my parents' oral histories: Mother's family represented the flat-land South, steeped in its magnolia myths, replete with Gorham sterling silver and Wedgwood china. My father's kinfolks spoke for the Appalachian South, where the pioneer spirit took root. In their War Between the States, the Cause was somebody else's business, and the war was a deadly struggle between neighbors. I could not belong completely to either of these Souths because I am inextricably a part of both. This duality of my childhood, a sense of having a foot in two cultures, gave me that sense of *otherness* that one often finds in writers: the feeling of being an outsider, observing one's surroundings, and looking even at personal events at one remove.

So much conflict; so much drama; and two sides to everything. Stories, I learned, involved character, and drama, and they always centered around irrevocable events that mattered.

In addition to personal histories set in Appalachia, I was given a sampling of my father's taste in literature: the romantic adventure tales of H. Rider Haggard and Edgar Rice Burroughs, and the frontier stories of Mark Twain and Bret Harte, and the sentimental surprise-ending works of Dickens and O. Henry. Add to that the poetry of

Benet, Tennyson, Whittier, and Longfellow. It is no wonder that, years later, when I was ready to be a published writer, I found that I had no aptitude for minimalism, despite studies in the contemporary trends in creative writing at my alma mater UNC Chapel Hill, and later at Virginia Tech, where I received my M.A. in English. I took all the courses in Victorian literature that the university offered, and it was there that I found my mentors.

My role model of a successful, important writer became Charles Dickens, not for his style, but for his philosophy. Charles Dickens wrote best sellers in order to change the world. Here's one example: In the mid-nineteenth century, child labor laws in Britain were virtually non-existent. Children worked twelve hour days in factories, were maimed in coal mines, and died of lung disease in their teens from work as chimney sweeps. No one seemed to care. For decades ministers and social reformers wrote earnest pamphlets reeling off the statistics of child mortality, and calling for child-protection laws. These pamphlets were mostly read by people who already agreed with the author; other ministers and social reformers who were working on pamphlets of their own. And nobody did anything to help the children. Then Charles Dickens wrote a book. It was a novel, about a little boy who suffered terribly in the workhouse: *David Copperfield.*

Then came *Oliver Twist*, with its grim picture of a child's life on the street in the slums of London. Those books became best-sellers in Great Britain, and within two years of their publication *the child labor laws of England were changed.* The general public, who had never bothered to read the informative pamphlets, wept for a little boy who existed only in a novel, and as an echo of the author's childhood. People became so outraged at the fate of these fictional children, that they demanded laws protecting child workers. First Dickens had to make people care; then he could persuade them to act. This is what

John Gardner later called "moral fiction," and I knew early on that I wanted my words to make a difference. Writing should do more than entertain.

Even the early comic novels that I wrote when I was in graduate school reflect this sense of purpose: that a good book should have a message. The books featuring forensic anthropologist Elizabeth MacPherson have been described as "Jane Austen with an Attitude" for the way that they blend social issues into the plots. In each of the early novels, the murder is committed by someone who is trying to protect an assumed cultural identity – not for greed, or revenge, or any of the usual motives. Cultural identity, I learned from my dual-culture childhood, is optional. The point of those novels is not to reveal "whodunit," but to satirize a pretentious segment of society: in *Highland Laddie Gone*, for example, the Scottish Wannabes at the Highland Games are lampooned. These satirical novels reflect the culture of my mother's South: the mannered society where appearances and social position matter. The dark and troubled world of the Ballad novels are the other South, drawn on my father's Appalachian heritage.

The idea of being a writer took root early in my consciousness. When I was seven, I announced that I was going to be a writer – even though I had to ask my parents how to spell about every third word of my compositions. I must have been nine when I heard the Irish song "Danny Boy" for the first time, and while I recognized the urgency and sadness in the song, I could not figure out where Danny was going, and why his father wasn't sure he'd ever seen him again. Unable to get any satisfactory answers on these points from the lyrics, I invented a story to explain the situation in the song. It has to do with a changeling being reclaimed from his human foster parents by the Irish fairies, but it wasn't a bad effort for the imagination of a nine-year old. I still think it might be a good children's book.

This attempt to make sense of the inexplicable by making up my own "legend" is still an occasional source of inspiration to my work, most notably in the novel *If Ever I Return, Pretty Peggy-O*, which began as an attempt to answer the question: "I wonder who lives in that house." *That house* is a stately white mansion set amid stately oaks on Highway 264 on the outskirts of Wilson, North Carolina. My parents lived in Greenville, North Carolina, and practically the only way to reach Greenville from points west was to take Highway 264, which meant that I had been driving past that white mansion for nearly twenty years: home for weekends from UNC Chapel Hill, back from my job as a newspaper reporter in Winston-Salem, and later back from the Virginia Blue Ridge, where my husband and I were attending graduate school at Virginia Tech.

In the spring of 1985 I was driving home by myself when I passed the big white house on Highway 264, and I said for at least the two hundredth time, "I wonder who lives in that house." I still don't know who really lives there: it isn't the sort of place that invites drop-in visits from inquisitive strangers. I decided to answer the question with my imagination. *"A woman lives in the house,"* I thought. *"She bought the house with her own money. She didn't marry to get the house, and she didn't inherit it. Who is she?"* A folksinger. She would have to have made a substantial amount of money to be able to buy the house, but in order to take up residence in a small Southern town, her career would have to be over.

A character began to take shape. This folksinger had attended UNC-Chapel Hill in the Sixties, as I had. She was still young-looking, a trim blonde woman in her early forties, who had once been a minor celebrity in folk music, but her popularity waned with the change in musical trends, so now she has bought the white mansion in the small Southern town, looking for a place to write new songs, so that she can stage a musical comeback, probably in Nashville. *She doesn't know anybody here,* I thought.

I had loved folk music when I was in college, and I had grown up listening to my father's mixture of Ernest Tubb and Francis Child, so I began to consider what songs this folksinger character might have recorded. Since I was alone in the car, I could sing my selections as I drove along. After a couple of Peter, Paul, and Mary tunes, I happened to recall an old mountain ballad called "Little Margaret." I was reminded of it, because I had heard Kentucky poet laureate Jim Wayne Miller sing it in a speech at Virginia Tech only a few weeks earlier. The song is a Child Ballad. It is four centuries old, and it is a ghost story. Little Margaret sees her lover William ride by with his new bride, and she vows to go to his house to say farewell, and then never to see him again. When she appears like a vision in the newlyweds' bed chamber that night, William realizes that he still loves her, and he goes to her father's house, asking to see her: *"Is Little Margaret in the house, or is she in the hall?"* He receives a chilling reply: *"Little Margaret's lying in her cold, black coffin with her face turned to the wall."*

I sang that verse a few times, because some instinct told me that the heart of my story was right there. The owner of the house is a folksinger. She has moved to a small town, where she doesn't know anybody, and one day she receives a postcard in the mail, with one line printed on the back: *"Is Little Margaret in the house, or is she in the hall?"* The folksinger's name is Margaret! The line would terrify her with its implied threat, and she would take the message personally, because her own name was in the line. Having sung the song many times in her career, she knows the next line: *"Little Margaret's lying in her cold, black coffin with her face turned to the wall."* I pictured her calling the local sheriff in a panic, and saying that someone is threatening her life, but the sheriff sees no threat in the line on the postcard. He tells her that the message is simply a prank. I thought: Suppose something or someone close to her is violently destroyed that night. Then she will know that the threat was serious. Then all she can do is wait for the next postcard to come, as she and the sheriff try to find out who is stalking her.

As I drove toward my parents' house, I followed the thread of the plot, so that by the time I reached Greenville, I knew who lived in that house, (which I had mentally relocated to east Tennessee), and I had the seeds of the first Ballad novel *If Ever I Return, Pretty Peggy-O.* That hour of inspiration was followed by several years of hard work, researching the high school reunions of Sixties' graduates, talking to Vietnam veterans, and interviewing law enforcement people, but the idea itself came from an old mountain song.

The theme of *If Ever I Return, Pretty Peggy-O* came from a more modern melody: the Doors' tune "Strange Days Have Tracked Us Down." I thought: Suppose *strange days* tracked everybody down one summer in an east Tennessee village. For the Baby Boomers it is their 20th high school reunion, forcing them to come to terms with their shortcomings; for the sheriff and his deputy, it is the memory of Vietnam, which haunts them both but for different reasons; and for Peggy Muryan, the once-famous folksinger, strange days track her down in the form of a stalker who still remembers her days of celebrity. For Appalachia itself, the *strange days* refer to the time when the traditional folkways began to be lost in the onslaught of the modern media culture. Child ballads gave way to the Top 40; quilts featured cartoon character designs; and the distinctiveness of the region began to erode as it was bombarded by outside influences. In each case *strange days* meant the Sixties.

Music is a continuous wellspring of creativity for me. When I was writing the subsequent Appalachian Ballad novels, I would make a sound track for each book before I began the actual process of writing. The CD, dubbed by me from tracks of albums in my extensive collection, would contain songs that I felt were germane to the themes of the book, and sometimes a song that I thought one of the characters might listen to, or a "theme song" for each of the main characters. Generally, the songs I use to focus my thinking do not appear in the novel itself; they are solely for my benefit, although I have thought of providing a "play list" in the epilogue to each book.

The sound track for *She Walks These Hills*, for example, is a mixture of Bluegrass, Scottish folk songs, and modern country music. It begins with the Don Williams recording of "Good Old Boys Like Me," a song that captures the character of Sheriff Spencer Arrowood in a few well-chosen lines: "...Those Williams boys, they still mean a lot to me: Hank and Tennessee." A "good old boy" who is able to appreciate both Hank Williams and Tennessee Williams has a blend of urbanity and traditionalism that typifies the rural Tennessee sheriff I wanted to create. The music of Deputy Joe LeDonne's is an acid rock tune from the Sixties, "Break on Through to the Other Side." A Vietnam vet, LeDonne listens only to recordings made in the late Sixties and early Seventies: Otis Redding, the Grateful Dead, Kris Kristofferson, Janis Joplin. Other songs on my home-made album for *She Walks These Hills* include: "Jamie Raeburn," a Scots folk song about a convict forced to leave his homeland; the Bluegrass standard "Fox on the Run," both theme tunes for the novel's escaped convict Harm Sorley, as well as "Poor Wayfaring Stranger;" "The Bounty Hunter" written and sung by North Carolina musician Mike Cross;

and a selection of hammered dulcimer recordings of traditional Scottish and Irish melodies.

When the CD is finished, I make one copy of it for my car, and another one for my office. Then during the months that I am researching, before I write a word of the book itself, I play the car tape whenever I am driving, so that I can absorb and internalize the sound and the themes of the novel-to-come. I suppose the music serves as both the means of directing my thoughts along the lines of motivation, characterization, and theme during the planning phase of the novel, and later for the creation of mood when I am in my study actually working on the book.

The songs I listen to also provide the titles for the Ballad novels. *If Ever I Return, Pretty Peggy-O* is a line from the Joan Baez recording of "Fenario," a minor key variation of a Scots folk song alternately called "The Bonnie Streets of Fyvie-O;" a line from the chorus of Danny Dill's 1959 folk revival tune "The Long Black Veil" is the source of the title of *She Walks These Hills*, and "The Rosewood Casket" is a late nineteenth century song, most recently popularized by Dolly Parton, Emmy Lou Harris, and Linda Ronstadt on their album *Trio*. As I write this essay, the novel I am working on is entitled *The Ballad of Frankie Silver*, after a song attributed to the first woman hanged for murder in North Carolina (in fact Frankie Silver did not write the song; she was almost certainly illiterate). I am also researching (still in the rather desultory fashion of one who is a long way from a plot) the Civil War in the Appalachian mountains, where the conflict was intensely personal, and there was no great Cause to illuminate the suffering. The song that I find myself listening to when I'm reading Appalachian Civil War material is the traditional tune "Rank Strangers;" surely that will be the title of the book, when I finally sit down to write it. I like the play on words, and the idea conveyed by the song that a civil war suddenly turns neighbors into strangers. The faux cowboy ballad "Ghost Riders in the Sky" is also on my Civil War soundtrack-in-progress. So far, I have no inkling as to why it's there.

I find that the more I write, the more fascinated I become with the idea of the past as prologue. I began the fourth Ballad novel, *The Rosewood Casket*, with a quote from Pinero: "I believe the future is simply the past entered through another gate." In order to make sense of the present, I look to incidents in the past, and I like to know where things came from, so that I can understand how they came to be what they are today. This sense of inquiry led me to read books on such diverse subjects as the legends of the Cherokee, mountain botany and ornithology, and the natural history of Appalachia.

In *The Rosewood Casket*, I wanted to talk about the passing of the land from one group to another, as a preface to the modern story of farm families losing their land to the developers in today's Appalachia. The voice of Daniel Boone is central to the novel's message, a reminder that the land inherited by the farm families was once taken from the Cherokee and the Shawnee. The novel begins with Cherokee wise woman Nancy Ward, in the last spring of her life, as she realizes that her people are about to lose the land that she tried so hard to preserve for them. As a reminder of that transience of ownership, in a passage in chapter one of *The Rosewood Casket*, I trace the passing of the land even farther back: to a time at the end of the last Ice Age, twelve thousand years ago.

Appalachia was a very different place at the end of the Ice Age, when the first humans are believed to have arrived in the mountains. The climate of that far-off time was that of central Canada today, too cold to support the oaks and hickories of our modern forests. Appalachia then was a frozen land of spruce and fir tree, but it was home to a wonderful collection of creatures: mastodons, saber-tooth tigers, camels, horses, sloths the size of pick-up trucks, and birds of prey with wingspans of twenty-five feet. The kingdom of ice that was Appalachia in 10,000 B.C. was their world, and they lost it to the first human settlers of the region, who hunted the beasts to extinction in only a few hundred years. Losing the land is an eternal process, I wanted to say. It seemed fitting to start with these early residents, as a reminder that even the Indians were once interlopers. The theme song for that book was "Will the Circle Be Unbroken?"

A scholarly publication on Appalachian geology provided me with one of the central themes of *She Walks These Hills*, a novel of intertwining journeys, past and present. An elderly convict escapes from the Northeast Correctional Center in Mountain City, Tennessee, and tries to make his way home through the same stretch of wilderness in which a Virginia Tech history professor is re-enacting the eighteenth century journey of a pioneer woman who escaped from captivity with the Shawnee. The climax of the novel is the convergence of all these epic journeys.

From a book by Dr. Kevin Dann, *Traces on the Appalachians: A History of Serpentine in America* (Rutgers University Press, 1988), I learned that the first journey was the journey made by the mountains themselves. A vein of a green mineral called serpentine forms its own subterranean "Appalachian Trail" along the mountains, stretching from north Georgia to the hills of Nova Scotia, where it seems to stop. This same vein of serpentine can be found in the mountains of western Ireland, where it again stretches north into Cornwall, Wales, Scotland, and the Orkneys, finally ending in the Arctic Circle. More than two hundred and fifty million years ago (before even fish existed yet) the mountains of Appalachia and the mountains of Great Britain fit together like a jigsaw puzzle. Continental drift pulled them apart, at the same time it formed the Atlantic Ocean. I thought this bit of geology was a wonderful metaphor for the journeys reflected in the book, and in a sociological way, it closed the circle. When our pioneer ancestors settled in the mountains because the land looked right, made them feel at home, they were right back in the same mountains they had left to come to America!

Because I do so much research for my novels, and because I like to include so many historical and scientific details in the narrative, people often ask me which comes first: the story or the research. I usually reply by quoting another favorite maxim of mine, one from Louis Pasteur, perhaps an unlikely source of inspiration for a Southern novelist, but his advice is sound for many disciplines. Pasteur said: "Chance favors the prepared mind." Much of my reading is non-fiction, particularly natural history, anthropology, and the sciences.

My reference shelves fill all the bookcases in my study, so that I have easy access to trail guides of the Cherokee National Park, field studies of birds and wildflowers, the poetry of Stephen Vincent Benet, the Toe River Valley Heritage book, several hundred volumes of folklore of Britain, and a host of other arcane volumes that I do not trust libraries to have in stock.

When I am reading subjects that have nothing to do with the book-in-progress, I am ostensibly reading for pleasure and relaxation, but I am always alert for new ideas. There is no telling when a chance sentence or an unexpected topic will trigger an association, or suggest a subject that can be put to use in one's work. I was reading a medical journal when I discovered Korsakov's Syndrome, the form of brain damage that affected escaped convict Harm Sorley in *She Walks These Hills*. I chose to afflict the character with that mental disorder in order to have him stuck in the past; Harm became a twentieth century version of Don Quixote, forever trapped in a better place and time than Now.

Once I used an idea from folklore that I understood only intuitively, and then later found the confirmation in a volume on Celtic beliefs. The theme for the second Ballad novel, *The Hangman's Beautiful Daughter,* was the idea of being "betwixt and between": to be caught in a liminal state between life and death. I found that each of the issues in the novel (the polluted river, the stillborn child, the country singer forced into retirement, the old woman with the Sight who talks to the dead, the hibernating groundhog; the young suicide who still contacts his grieving sister) involved someone or something lingering on the threshold between life and death, reaching both ways. My feeling that this theme was integral to the mountain culture was instinctive. After I completed the novel, I found the justification for this theme of liminality in a book discussing Celtic beliefs. In *Ravens and Black Rain: The Story of Highland Second Sight* (Constable, London 1985), Scottish writer Elizabeth Sutherland says:

"Celtic mysteries occurred in twi-states between night and day, in dew that was neither rain nor river, in mistletoe that was not a plant or a tree, in the trance state that was neither sleep nor waking. The Christian sense of duality~ good and bad, right and wrong, black and white, body and soul~ was unknown to the Druid. The key to Celtic philosophy is the merging of dark and light, natural and supernatural, conscious and unconscious. The sithean themselves existed in this twi-state, beings who dwelled between one world and another, creatures who were neither men nor gods." (Sutherland, p.26.)

There it was. The liminality that I kept insisting belonged in the narrative of *The Hangman's Beautiful Daughter* was part of the world view held by the ancestors of the mountain people for thousands of years. Although I hadn't been sure why I'd felt compelled to put the concept of liminality into the text, now the reason was clear. I was describing people of Scots descent, keeping to the old ways, and this *border* concept is central to their world view. The scene in the novel in which Nora Bonesteel gathers balm of Gilead plants for making medicine reflected this ancient philosophy. (But I wrote this passage *before* I read Sutherland's work.)

Here is the Celtic belief in liminality as expressed by Appalachian wise woman Nora Bonesteel in chapter ten of *The Hangman's Beautiful Daughter.*

When Nora was a girl, a few of the old women had claimed that balm of Gilead ought to be harvested at dawn or dusk, but these days she dispensed with that part of the ritual. Early mornings and evenings were colder than mid-day, and she was too old to brave a chill for the sake of rough magic. She understood the logic behind the stricture, though. There was a power in the borders of things: in the twilight hours that separated day from night; in rivers that divided lands; in the caves and wells that lay suspended between the earth and the underworld. The ancient holy days had been the divisions between summer and winter, and that border in time created a threshold for other things; that was why ghosts and goblins were thought to roam on Halloween and Beltane. The mountains themselves were a border, Nora thought. They separated the placid coastal plain from the flatland to the west, and there was magic in them.

I read non-fiction incessantly, always trolling for some relevant thought or fact that will add a grace note to the next story. I keep hardbound notebooks for possible future novels, each one labeled with the working title. When I see an article, a quote, or a phrase that might pertain to the subject of this future book, I copy it onto a blank page in the scrapbook. I have discovered through bitter experience that it is much easier to stockpile things you may never use than it is to try to track down an article or a reference several years after you've seen it, when your memory of where it can be found is no longer reliable. The prepared mind saves me much time and energy in the long run, and the background reading that I have done has triggered associations and brought other facets of the story into focus, giving my work a scope and texture that it would not otherwise have.

I read. I study. I interview people who are experts in the subject of the current work. I have hiked the Appalachian Trail with a naturalist, done laps on the track at Lowe's Motor Speedway with a NASCAR driver, and explored country music with Skeeter Davis. I researched wood-working with a master dulcimer-maker, and I have sat in Tennessee's electric chair. I try to write interesting, compelling stories, *because I think it is the duty of a fiction writer to entertain, but: beyond the reader's concern for the characters, I want there to be an overlay of significance about the issues and the ambiguities that we face in Appalachia today.* In my novels I want there to be truth, and an enrichment of the reader's understanding of the mountains and their people. I have been known to warn people not to read my books with their brains in neutral. Dickens again: "Never be inducted to suppose that I write merely to amuse or without an object." I have a mission.

Appalachia is still trying to live down the stereotypical "backwoods" view of the region presented in the media. I think one of the best ways to combat this negative portrayal is to educate the general reader about the real character of the region, and particularly about the history and origins of Appalachia and its people, both culturally and environmentally. Like Charles Dickens, I think that in order to win hearts and minds, one must reach the greatest possible number of people, and so I am pleased when my novels make the *New York Times* best seller list, because that means that millions of people have been exposed to my point of view. Millions of people watched *The Dukes of Hazard*: surely the opposite opinion deserves equal time.

I am passing along the songs, the stories, and the love of the land to people who did not have a chance to acquire such things from heritage or residence. Perhaps my own theme song ought to be the one Joan Baez recorded on an early album called *One Day at A Time*: "Carry It On."

Carry it on.

A Novelist Looks at the Land

The strongest element in fiction set in the mountain South is a sense of place. That connection to the land is the key to understanding the people who settled here, those who are drawn to live here now, and those who cannot leave. In my Ballad novels I try both to celebrate the land, and to understand its power over those who have become a part of it.

The first member of my family to settle in America was my five-times great-grandfather Malcolm McCourry, a Scotsman who left a law practice in New Jersey in 1790, took a new young wife, raised a second family and homesteaded in a log cabin in the wildwood until his death in 1829 – a sojourn in the wilderness lasting longer than his tenure as a lawyer on the eastern seaboard.

He must have felt at home in the mountain fastness of western North Carolina. What he never knew was that in a geologic sense, he was back home. In *The Songcatcher*, my novel based on Malcolm McCourry's life, the central theme was provided by a scholarly publication on Appalachian geology. *In Traces on the Appalachians: A History of Serpentine in America* (Rutgers University Press, 1988), geologist Kevin Dann writes that the first Appalachian journey was the one made by the mountains themselves.

The proof of this can be found in a vein of a green mineral called serpentine which forms its own subterranean "Appalachian Trail" along America's eastern mountains, stretching from north Georgia to the hills of Nova Scotia, where it seems to stop. This same vein of serpentine can be found in the mountains of western Ireland, where it again stretches north into Cornwall, Wales, Scotland, and the

Orkneys, finally ending in the Arctic Circle. More than two hundred and fifty million years ago (before even fish existed yet) the mountains of Appalachia and the mountains of Great Britain fit together like a jigsaw puzzle. Continental drift pulled them apart, at the same time it formed the Atlantic Ocean.

The mountains' family connection to Britain reinforced what I had felt about the migration patterns of the early settlers. People forced to leave a land they loved come to America. Hating the flat, crowded eastern seaboard, they head westward on the Wilderness Road until they reach the wall of mountains. They follow the valleys south-southwest down through Pennsylvania, and finally find a place where the ridges rise, where you can see vistas of mountains across the valley. The Scots, the Irish, the Welsh, the Cornishmen – all those who had lives along the other end of the serpentine chain – to them this place must have looked right. Must have felt right. Like home. *And they were right back in the same mountains they had left behind in Britain.*

Perhaps it isn't a unique experience in nature, this yearning for a place to which one is somehow connected. After years in the vast ocean salmon return to spawn in the same small stream from whence they and their forebears came; Monarch butterflies make the journey from the eastern seaboard to the same field in Mexico that had been the birthplace of the previous generation. The journey there and back again is unchanging, but each generation travels only one way. Is it really so strange that humans might feel some of this magnetism toward the land itself?

If you go looking for the serpentine chain in Britain, the best place to find it is on the Lizard, a peninsula in Cornwall between Falmouth and Penzance that is the southernmost tip of England. There at Kynance Cove you can see the cliffs of magnesium-rich serpentine, and the chain of rocks in the bay that marks the path to Ireland's link on the great geologic chain. The other end of the serpentine chain follows the Appalachian Mountains from Alabama to the tip of New Brunswick. How wonderful, I think, that the people who loved those mountains in Britain found them again when they came to settle in this country.

My office sits perched on the edge of the ridge so that from my window I can see green meadows far below, and folds of multi-colored hills stretching away to the clouds in the distance. It could be any century at all in that vista, which is just the view one needs to write novels set in other times. I tell myself I don't want to live anywhere else, but every year or two, I make my way back to Britain, and I spend a few weeks wandering around the west of Ireland, or the coves of Cornwall, or the cliffs of Scotland – an ocean away from home, but still connected by the serpentine chain.

The Celts and the Appalachians

From a lecture by Sharyn McCrumb

My favorite story illustrating the character of the Appalachian Celtic people is an incident that happened in 1960 in the mountains of western North Carolina.

If you were on the East Coast in 1960, you may remember that it was a terrible winter. In North Carolina in particular, the March weather was fierce. That month it snowed every Monday. That's much more snow than North Carolina usually gets. With this steady fall, the snow did not melt. It just kept piling up and piling up. The North Carolina transportation department did not have the resources to deal with a snowfall of this magnitude. The accumulation was so great that back in the western mountains of the state, the roads, especially unpaved rural back roads, never got cleared and soon became impassible. People who lived in cabins way back in the coves couldn't get out. Because many of them were elderly, the Red Cross was called in to try to get help to these elderly citizens trapped back there, deep in the mountains.

Two Red Cross workers had heard about an old woman in her eighties who lived in a cabin way back in the hills, and they volunteered to take a jeep to bring help to her. The two volunteers drove up the ice-bound road as far as they could, abandoned the jeep when the road became impassable, got out snow shoes, wrestled them on, and helped each other tramp through the waist-deep snow until, finally, they saw the little curl of chimney smoke up on the ridge that told them they'd found her. They managed to hike to the cabin on the top of the hill, stomped up on the porch, and rapped on the door. Finally the old lady opened it.

The rescuers announced proudly. "We're from the Red Cross." "Oh honey," she replied. "It has been such a hard winter, I don't think I can help you this year."

That's us: proud, independent, and willing to go through a good bit of hardship.

(N.B. I think that old lady knew exactly why those Red Cross workers had come, but she was employing the culture's deadpan sense of humor, and also gently inferring that she had no intention of accepting charity.)

My family settled the western North Carolina mountains in 1790. The story of my family origin is something I learned only when I was researching my novel *The Ballad of Frankie Silver* (Dutton, May 1998). I was tracking down the histories of the people of Mitchell County as part of the research for my novel about Frankie Silver, the first woman hanged for murder in North Carolina. Frankie Silver came from Mitchell County. In the course of my research there, I discovered an enormous number of cousins. One of them, a professor of theology at Duke University who has done a lot of our family research, was able to tell me about our first ancestor who came and settled in the mountains. It was a better story than most of mine, so a few years later I told his story in *The Songcatcher.*

Malcolm McCourry was born on the island of Islay, off the west coast of Scotland. In the 1751, when Malcolm was a child of ten, he was kidnapped from Islay, and made to serve as a crew man on a sailing ship. He spent the rest of his childhood on the ship, but when he was in his late teens he was either let go or escaped, and he made his way to Morristown, New Jersey. There he read the law with an attorney and set up a law practice. During the American Revolution, he served as quartermaster with the Morris Militia. After the war, when many soldiers were given land grants as a reward for military service, Malcolm McCourry took his land grant in the mountains of western North Carolina. You understand that land grants aren't given for places like downtown Baltimore, but for some remote territory that no one else wants to homestead - in this case, Indian land. Malcolm took his grant, moved south, and settled in what-is-now Mitchell County. I'm descended from Malcolm McCourry, and from another 18th century pioneer family: the Arrowoods (pronounced *Arwood*).

Malcolm would have come to America around 1760, a time when a great deal of the Celtic migration was happening. People came along in the 1600s and 1700s, and especially after 1746 when the Jacobite rising in Scotland failed. That was the last attempt to restore a Stuart and a Catholic - Charles Edward Stuart, known as Bonnie Prince Charlie - to the throne. The Highland Clearances followed: a forced exit of both Jacobite rebels and of crofters driven from the land to make room for sheep. The political effect of the Clearances is probably not as important as the cultural effect. What the English did, after they defeated the Scots, was to change the entire culture. They wanted to anglicize Scotland, anglicize Celtic Britain. The whole lifestyle of Scotland was foreign to the English way of doing things. In Scotland the laird or chief and his extended family, which was called the clan, was the focal point of the social order, and the pastoral economy of tending herds necessitated a tribal lifestyle. The English and the Celts even differed on the use of surnames. The Scots custom of taking as your surname your father's first name, wasn't going to work for the English bureaucracy. One's patronym would change with every generation, which would muddle the tax people, and the lawyers, and central government. The British wanted things a little more regimented.

The Highland Clearances were often effected by taking a sailing ship up to an island, telling the people in the cottages that they had until sundown to get on the ship, and, at sundown, burning the cottages. The ship then sailed for America, and wherever it docked, the people were let out. That was it. Go find a home. So, between 1763 and 1775, more than 20,000 people from the Scottish Highlands came to the colonies or to Canada, somewhere in North America, and settled. In 1775, the British banned emigration to the soon-to-be United States. We know why: the American Revolution. People might arrive, grab a musket, then face back the other way – especially the Celts.

The first US Census, in 1790, is not particularly helpful for modern researchers, because only the head of the household is listed by name. The wife and any children, dependents, or household members such as servants, are listed merely by sex and age, which is not useful in determining the name of your great-grandmother. However, it did list the surname of the household. The people who analyze sociological data say that by 1790, 75% of New England was Anglo-Saxon, and more that 75% of Pennsylvania and the lands to the south and west of that state were Celtic. This disparity established a profound cultural dissonance that continues to resound to this day. The real cultural dissonance though seems to me to be between the mountain people and those who live in the flatlands on either side of those mountains – and in the 18th century, according to census records, those flatlanders were mostly Anglo-Saxon.

There is some argument about the identity of the people we call "Appalachian." Scholars have noted that, because they came down from the north, they are not Southern, but are more like New

Englanders. Certainly the same ethnic groups settled the mountain regions in both places, and you'll find the same fiddle tunes, folk tales, and quilt patterns all along those mountains, and also in eastern Canada. The Appalachian mountains form a barrier between settlers there and the eastern seaboard, thus making a "vertical" culture, in which east Tennessee and western North Carolina may well resemble, say, Vermont, more than they do the other portions of their own states.

The Appalachian Mountains form a barrier which extends south/southwest all along the Eastern seaboard. The easiest way to get into the mountains is not to start at the coast of, say, Charleston (SC) or Richmond (VA) or Wilmington (NC), and go due west. The best way is to get into the mountain chain around Pennsylvania, and work your way south at an angle, following the mountain passes between the ridges. The migration patterns do reflect this. The people who settled the mountains moved down from the north, going south-southwest. The people who settled the coastal plain landed there in the first place, or else they started in the mid-Atlantic and went west until they got to Statesville, North Carolina or to some inconvenient place where the mountain barrier was difficult to pass, so they quit, and either stayed there or turned back east. They didn't want to live in the mountains, anyway. The people who did want to live there were the people who were used to a Highland sort of existence before.

When I was writing *She Walks These Hills*, I studied the geology of the region, because connections between Britain and Appalachia interest me, culturally and any other way. One of the most delightful things I learned came from a textbook by Kevin Dann. (*Traces Along the Appalachians: The History of Serpentine in America*). The book was published by Rutgers University Press in a print run probably large enough to fill his entire Christmas card list, but I managed to get hold of a copy. What Dann had done was to analyze the mountain structure, taking into account plate tectonics, orogeny, and continental drift, and to conclude that the mountains of Appalachia and the mountains of Britain were once joined together.

The Appalachians start in north Alabama, (you can see them encircling the race track at Talladega), and the mountain chain runs up through Georgia, through South and North Carolina, Tennessee, Virginia, West Virginia, Pennsylvania, and New York. *(I realize that the stereotypes stop about Pittsburgh, but the mountain chain itself, and in many respects the culture, extends through New York and New England and finally ends in the Canadian province of New Brunswick.)* There, at Campbelltown, the Appalachians stop. If you took core samples in the Atlantic, you wouldn't find that vein of serpentine, which is the genetic DNA of the Appalachian mountains, this green mineral that rises in Georgia, follows the chain to Canada, and then quits... until it reappears in the west of Ireland. You've skipped the Atlantic Ocean, which is recent by geological standards. The mountains of Connemara contain the same vein of serpentine as our mountains. The serpentine chain extends into through Cornwall, up through Wales into the north of England, and into Scotland, the Orkney Islands, and finally ends in the Arctic Circle.

I thought that geologic discovery was a wonderful reinforcement of what I had sensed about the migration patterns. Here are people who left a land that they loved, that they were known to love - the whole idea of *nature* and *place* was treasured by the Celtic people - and they were forced to resettle. They come to this country. They look around. The eastern seaboard is crowded, and filled with exactly the sort of people they didn't get along with back home. (If you want to understand Appalachia, the movie to rent is *Braveheart*.) Boston, New York, Philadelphia, Baltimore, Richmond... all are too flat, too hot, and people live too close together. The settlers keep heading south-southwest, and finally they get to a place where the ridges rise, where you can see the mountains across broad valleys in the distance, and it looks right, and it feels right. Like home. Like the place they left. With them they brought those fiddle tunes, quilt patterns, folk tales, all kinds of wonderful things that, although they've changed over time, still show the family resemblance, as there is between cousins. *And these settlers never knew that they were right back in the same mountains they had left behind in Britain.*

One summer I took a six-week-version of today's lecture with a professor of folklore who is the model for the real Nora Bonesteel. We went to Ireland, rented a car, and proceeded to put 1800 miles on that car in a country about the size of Maryland. We went to all the pre-Christian sites we could find, to all the different ruins that we could find, and we looked for connections between the culture we knew in the mountains of the South and the Irish culture. If you are interested in going yourself, there are places I'd recommend.

One is the Craiganouwen Project in County Clare, an hour or so from the Shannon airport, near Quin. There a group of archaeologists have recreated the different types of dwellings that people lived in from prehistoric times through the middle ages in Ireland. They constructed beehive huts that the Celts used and the *crannogs*, man-made islands that the ancient Irish used to protect themselves from enemies. They would build an artificial island in the middle of a lake. They'd put the beehive huts out on this island, which was built by piling rocks into the lake, and finally covering the projecting mound with dirt - not a quick process. When it was finished, the crannog-dwellers would put down a path of stepping stones leading from the shore to the island. The rocks were slightly submerged so that they couldn't be seen, so that anyone who wanted to cross over to the island had to memorize the route. The theory is that when you're being chased by the enemy of the month, you go running through the woods, get to the lake, skip across to the island, and mount a defensive with arrows or spears while the enemy is forced to pause and pick its way along, searching for the submerged path of rocks.

If you drive around Ireland, you won't see the ancient beehive huts. They've been gone for thousands of years, but you will see lots of little islands in Irish lakes. They are not natural formations. They were put there. If you excavate, as archaeologists are doing, you will find traces of that ancient civilization. The Craiganouwen Project, not wanting to destroy an actual archaeological site, built its own island on a lake in an estate and constructed a nice new beehive hut using wattle and daub, weaving willows together. You can visit it. Occasionally a fellow dressed in hides will greet you and answer the odd question or two. Also on display is a log canoe made by burning the wood until you get a dugout boat. In the forest, the project builders have erected a palisaded ring fort, huts surrounded by a tall wooden fence much like the basic army forts built along our own frontier. The most ingenious thing about the ring fort was its escape route. There was only one gate – apparently the only way in and out of the stockade. But if the enemy is at the gate, the villagers could go into one of the huts. Concealed in the earth floor there is a trap door. Pull it up, go down the ladder, and you find a little tunnel that comes out in the woods. It's a back door. So while the enemy is beating on the front gate trying to break in, the villagers make their escape. Assuming you closed the trap door behind you, they might never guess how you got away. (On a later visit, my nine-year-old son loved this.)

Finally there is Tim Severn's reconstruction of the boat that, according to legend, was used by St. Brendan on his voyage to the new world in the Sixth century. He made it! He also wrote the first bestseller when he got home. His book told the story of his voyage in a coracle or leather-covered boat. Many scholars scoffed at this legend, saying St. Brendan couldn't possibly have reached America in a leather-covered boat a thousand years before Columbus. But Tim Severn sailed from that same place on the Dingle Peninsula, Brendan Bay, where St. Brendan is said to have departed, in the same kind of boat, and Tim Severn made it to Canada. And I say, if Tim Severn did it, St. Brendan did it. (When my daughter's third grade class had Columbus week, and everyone had to do a project commemorating the voyage to the Americas, Laura, who'd been to the project with me, produced her photos and map, and gave a lecture on St. Brendan: "How the Irish Discovered America.")

Two other places I recommend for studying American-Irish connections are the Bunratty Folk Park and the Ulster Folk Park: they are similar reconstructions of the past. The Bunratty Folk Park, in County Clare, has constructed replicas of eighteenth and nineteenth century farm houses, manor houses, and little villages. They are artificial, but reasonably accurate. In Ulster, the folk park features actual dwellings, located throughout Ireland, and then moved to the Folk Park for preservation. Thus you can see the real buildings there, just south of Belfast.

My mother-in-law made this trip with us. Her ancestors had come over from Sligo three generations ago, during the potato famine. She had always wanted to go back to Ireland, but part of our itinerary on that trip was Ulster, and she was terrified of Northern Ireland. She updated her will, and told everybody goodbye before we left, vastly amusing the real Nora Bonesteel. As we headed north, through Donegal, Charlotte said to my mother-in-law, "Nancy, we're coming up on Northern Ireland, you'd better get ready." Nancy rummaged for her passport, found the rental car papers, prepared to convince the armed guards that we were just harmless tourists (she figures that with me and Charlotte along the guards are going to need convincing) and presently we come up to this little toll booth off to one side of the road. There's a stout fellow in a sleeveless shirt standing out front, and as I slow down to 35 miles per hour, he snaps a friendly wave, I snap one back. And that's the Irish border crossing. (Grimly, and not amused, my mother-in-law spent the new few miles putting away the passports, the car rental papers, etc.) In Ulster, Charlotte and I saw no one more dangerous than ourselves.

Northern Ireland was wonderful. In Armagh you can visit the site of Navan, the Camelot of Ireland, home to Cuchulain and the cattle raiders of Cooley, all the Irish heroes like Ossian (pronounced *O'Sheen*). The court of the king was at Navan, and their visitor center has one of the best audiovisual programs I've ever seen.

It occurred to me on this trip that one might discover over there a folk song or a quilt pattern, and think, *"Aha, this familiar bit that I know from back home must have come from Ireland,"* but file this story away as a cautionary tale. We were going through the Ulster Folk Park looking at things like cabins because Charlotte contends (and she's right) that you can look at a cabin on our frontier – and certainly at the barns – and tell by the architecture where its builders came from. The structure of the rooms, and the building techniques, are clues to whether those who settled there were German, Irish, English: every ethnic group had its own style. People brought the old ways with them to the New World, and they continued to use them. We were looking at the patterns in the Ulster Folk Park to see what we can learn, when we reached the 19th century section.

We saw a little urban house that dated from 1890's Belfast. All the dwellings were furnished with period pieces, sofas, chairs, clocks, and so on. When my mother-in-law spotted a carriage clock on the mantelpiece, she recalled that her grandmother had owned a clock just like it, so she thought she was really on to something about the origin of a family heirloom. Her Irish ancestors had settled in western Pennsylvania, north of Pittsburgh. She wanted to know all about this Irish clock. The curator came and, when she asked him where the clock came from, he replied that it had come from western Pennsylvania. Many such clocks had been made there, he said, and in the late 19th century they had been sent back to Ireland by emigrant relatives. So I'm glad we asked instead of jumping to conclusions. Sometimes the transmission of cultures goes in the opposite direction from the one you were expecting.

Quite a number of scholars that I know are interested in all these cultural connections. Dr. Elizabeth Fine, head of the Appalachian Studies Program at Virginia Tech, gives a wonderful one-hour lecture that she has yet to put into print. I keep urging her to write a book about it. Dr. Fine takes quilt patterns and traces them back several thousand years. For example, she will show you a photograph of a quilt and then display a photograph of a rock from the Orkney Islands bearing the same pattern. What she contends (and a moment's thought will show you the logic), is that the quilters have long forgotten why they do particular patterns like the log cabin or the bear claw, or the wedding ring, or some intricate design, but that originally all these patterns were luck symbols, symbols of magic from an older civilization. Think about it: if you're making a coverlet to put over your loved one in the dark, and if you come from a time when people believed in demons and spirits, of course you're going to put symbols of protection on this blanket. That's why we have quilt patterns. I'm delighted that scholars are looking into so many aspects of this ancient heritage. (Years later, I put that concept about quilt magic in my novel

Ghost Riders, which is about the Civil War in the North Carolina mountains.)

The songs, even songs that we don't think of as being Scottish or Irish, sneak up on you. We know ballads that like "The Rising of the Moon" or "Barbara Allen," come from the British Isles. But consider the origins of other familiar folk songs, often assumed to be authentic American tunes. "The Bard of Armargh" - we call it "The Streets of Laredo." The Irish version predates our cowboy song by one hundred years. Quite a lot of songs are like that. In *If Ever I Return, Pretty Peggy-O*, I mention a song called "The Knoxville Girl," which was originally the Irish ballad "The Wexford Girl." When a similar murder case took place in Tennessee, the ballad-maker changed the locality of the borrowed song. Another ballad whose origin surprised me was one I knew in the 1960's when Peter, Paul, and Mary recorded it. The song, set in Kentucky, is called "The Lily of the West." I knew that in the early 1800's, the west was Kentucky. (It keeps moving.) For instance, when it was written, *The Last of the Mohicans* was a perfectly good western set in New York state. But "The Lily of the West" begins, *"When first I came to Louisville, some pleasure there to find..."* The girl in the song was a dance hall girl called Flora, the Lily of the West. Last summer, I went into a pub in County Clare, and there was someone singing, *"When first I came to Ireland..."* and the girl in his song was Flora, the Lily of the West. I thought: "Wait a minute, that girl's from Kentucky," but, no, she's from the *west*, originally meaning the west of Ireland, County Clare, Connemara, Galway, all still called The West. In the 1600's when Cromwell was destroying Ireland, the place to go for a dangerous time was to the wild west, *the west of Ireland.* Then in the 1700's, the concept of the wild west changed to mean the eastern seaboard of North America, where you could have adventures and fight Indians like the Shawnee.

By the 1800's, danger receded to Kansas, then to Colorado, then Arizona. Today the West may be Australia. Just wait, it'll be back.

My Ballad novels point out that the Appalachian stereotype comes from a time when Appalachia was "The West." In *The Rosewood Casket*, Daniel Boone's experiences are contrasted with events that are taking place today.

Speech patterns: the cadence of a Tennessee accent has that same lilt found in Irish speech. In *The Story of English*, a book and a video made in the 1980's, Cratis Williams of Appalachian State University talks about being able to place people according to where their ancestors came from by listening to their pronunciation of certain key words. He says some of these regional speech patterns transfer. So do some of the words, like *poke* for paper bag, common to Tennessee and common to Scotland generations ago. To redd, a verb, as in "to redd the room." Nobody in Minnesota's going to understand that, but it will be understood in Tennessee, and in Scotland. It's one of those key words...actually, it is Danish in origin, so maybe they would understand it in Minnesota. "Redd" in Danish is still used to mean clear-cutting timber.

American square dancing is very similar to Scottish or Irish country dancing.

Folk customs from Britain are still remembered on this side of the Atlantic, although they are now forty or fifty years out of date since Appalachia, like everywhere else, has CNN and other homogenizing forces at work to obscure the past. People who were old when I was a child would remember customs like telling the bees when someone dies, or putting a cloth over the mirror, or putting a little ball of salt on the window sill in the home of the deceased. All these are ancient traditions that go all the way back to Celtic Britain.

"The Long Black Veil," the origin of my book title *She Walks These Hills*, is not an old ballad, although it sounds like one. It was written in 1959 by Nashville songwriter Danny Dill. It's a kind of faux cowboy ballad: it sounds like one but it isn't. I found a wonderful version of "The Long Black Veil" that I play sometimes in my lectures, and I love to ask people in Appalachia who they think is singing. When I play this in Appalachian Study lectures, Willie Nelson gets the most votes, but people often suggest that the song is being performed by a local, non-professional singer. It's Mick Jagger of The Rolling Stones. This Mick Jagger recording of an American song has managed to fool professors of linguistics. I was very proud of him. I found a scholar who did her Ph.D. in Kentucky speech patterns, and when she heard it, she said "Well, that's not a professional singer, it's probably your uncle and you stuck a microphone in his face." She thought it was the real, genuine, Appalachian article. Finally, we were so puzzled by Mick Jagger's ability to sound authentic that we faxed Hodder, my London publisher, to ask "Where's that Jagger boy from?" They replied, "We think he's from Kent, but his mother's Australian. That probably explains it." I don't think that it does explain it. I expect what's happened is that Jagger had hung out for so many years as a professional musician with Willie Nelson, Johnny Cash, and so on – and he's an extraordinarily good mimic – that I think he picked up the accent. Trust me, his vowel sounds are perfect! That's my favorite recording of "The Long Black Veil," the one by Mick Jagger.

One of the reasons that I write the books to explain the Appalachian lifestyle is to combat the hillbilly stereotype, this whole "*Deliverance* was a documentary" type of thinking. At first, I thought that people just bought into L'il Abner – Al Capp spent an entire 72 hours in the mountains before he made a living from his cartoon stereotype – or *The Dukes of Hazzard*, which is Hollywood getting everything wrong. But I found that stereotyped thinking went back farther than that. Let me tell you about where some of the customs came from and what they mean.

In some cases, I wrote my books before I found out where the custom in question came from. There is a tradition in the mountains – and here again, thirty or forty years ago it was probably more necessary than now – called "helloing the house," which means one doesn't just approach a house and knock on the door, the visitor calls out first to announce his presence. In rural areas, you let people know you are coming. In this passage from *The Rosewood Casket*, Frank Whitescarver, the evil realtor in East Tennessee is trying to buy the farm from a family because the father is dying and the realtor realizes that none of the boys wants to come back and take over the land.

"He parked his Jeep Cherokee, noting the old truck and the other late-model car, and hoping the latter wasn't paid for. He helloed the house. He probably didn't need to with a younger generation of town boys in residence, but it was a habit worth keeping in the wilder parts of the mountains. People didn't like you to sneak up on them. A holdover from who knew what terrible times in the past. Revenue men, armed for a raid, perhaps, in the early part of the century. Or Civil War guerillas who turned the war in the southern mountains into a house-to-house feud, stealing livestock and ambushing the householders. You might even trace their wariness of strangers back to Scotland, the Rising of 1745, when the Duke of Cumberland sent his soldiers into the Highlands to kill the Jacobites–that is, anyone they could find. Many of the ones who hid–who distrusted strangers, and therefore survived– ended up here. The lessons of the past would not desert them easily. They distrusted trespassers instinctively. Frank didn't blame them. Even today, a trespasser might be a hunter who would shoot your cow by mistake, or a tourist who figured that the whole state was a theme park, open to the public. He had learned to smile broadly, and to use the front path."

That's helloing the house. One of the places that gave rise to it was Scotland after the Jacobite Rising when any stranger could kill you. Another source was in Ireland. The Irish penal laws were pretty instructive in not trusting your fellow men. These came after the Battle of the Boyne in 1690. The English decided that "they wanted the Irish to become insignificant slaves, fit for nothing but to hew wood and draw water."

So they barred the Catholics from the Army, the Navy, the law, commerce, and from every civic activity.

"No Catholic could vote, hold any office under the Crown, or purchase land. Catholic estates were dismembered by an enactment saying that at the death of a Catholic owner, the land must be divided among all his sons, not given to the oldest son," which meant that in three or four generations, a great landholder's descendants have become a bunch of small farmers. Education was made almost impossible since Catholics could not attend nor keep schools, nor send their children to be educated abroad. Priest hunting was considered to be a sport. So, the old families disappeared, the old estates were broken up, and no one could be trusted.

"His religion made him an outlaw. In the Irish House of Commons, the Irish peasant was described as 'the common enemy'. To whom could he look for redress. To his landlord? Almost invariably an alien conqueror. To the law? Not when every person connected with the law from jailer to judge was a Protestant who regarded him as the common enemy. And so he learned to take the law into his own hands, to keep his own business secret, to distrust strangers. These were dangerous lessons for any government to compel its subjects to learn, and a dangerous habit of mind for any nation to acquire." [*The Great Hunger.*]

We see the ramifications still, hundreds of years later, hundreds of miles from Ireland.

The other thing that the Irish and Scots share with their Appalachian descendants is love of land. Before the potato famine, very few Irish emigrated. In a contemporary account of the 1845 famine when conditions had become severe, the Earl of Derby underscores this love of country. He wrote: "Only during the famine did the Irish immigrants leave the country willingly, without the weeping and wailing, the shrieks of anguish, the keening as for the dead which could be witnessed in the west of Ireland at the departure of the immigrants." They hated to go. I picked up on this, not by knowing that it was something we brought with us, but by seeing how people felt about the Appalachian mountains. In a scene in *The Hangman's Beautiful Daughter,* on a Saturday before Christmas, Sheriff Spencer Arrowood is out on a hillside near the railroad tracks. There's a custom called "The Santa Claus Train" in which the coal companies who owned so much of the land and the resources in the mountains, get together a bunch of presents, load them on a train, and run that train a hundred miles or more through coal country, throwing the gifts off to the children waiting along the tracks. Spencer is there to keep order and to make sure no one gets hurt. In this passage, the sheriff is looking at the people he sees waiting there on the tracks for the Santa Claus Train.

"Spencer adjusted his brown Stetson and strolled down to the track. The steel rails stretched away between the cuts in the mountain pasture land, curving out of sight at the bend where the forest began. His boots crunched on the gravel siding as he leaned out to look along the length of track facing east. All was still. He turned and waved to the crowd camped on the hill. Some of them had brought blankets to sit on; others stood and talked, cigarettes dangling from their fingers, as shrieking blond children chased each other through the clumps of people and into the weeds.

There was a sameness to them, he thought, scanning the faces. Many of the women were overweight from a lifetime on the diet of the poor. The deep-fried and starchy foods that are both filling and cheap make pasty complexions and lumpish bodies. The men were short and gaunt, a combination of ancestral genetics and poor nutrition. Beer and cigarettes in lieu of vegetables and jogging didn't help any, either. But they were honest people, and if there was work to be had, they'd put in long hours without a murmur.

People he knew from Knoxville and from the flatlands were always saying how great the house prices were in east Tennessee, and how cheap it was to live in the mountains, but Spencer reckoned that living in the mountains cost most of those people on the hillside ten years of their lives. And maybe a future for their children. But they wouldn't leave~not for jobs or love. Those that did leave sickened in exile in the ugly cities of the Midwest, pining for the hills of home. Even people who weren't poor, like himself or Dallas Stuart's young law partner, J.W. Lyon, could make more money and advance their careers by moving elsewhere, but they continued to stay in the shadows of the mountains. Why can't we just get out of these hills? He wondered for the thousandth time. Why are we so willing to sacrifice so much to live in this beautiful place? If this were the Garden of Eden, God couldn't drive us out of here with a flaming sword. We'd sneak back when the angel wasn't looking.

The sad thing was that the poverty wasn't natural to the region. The livestock business had thrived before the chestnut blight, and just to the north of Hamelin, lay land that bore the richest deposits of anthracite coal in the world. You could stand by this railroad track at any hour of any day you chose and watch a mile-long coal train hauling the natural resources away. The coal mines weren't locally owned, and they didn't put much back into local taxes, either. The mine owners could afford lawyers and lobbyists to see to that. Spencer had once read that 90 percent of the state of West Virginia was owned by absentee landlords.

The coal companies would be running the train today; the only one of the year that didn't haul coal. At least they made this gesture; offered a little money to the people. But maybe if things had been different politically, there wouldn't have to be a train like this."

I thought that was ironic. If West Virginia, just by itself, seceded from the United States, it could be the fifth richest industrial nation in the world. But as it is, all the minerals are hauled away, and once a year they bring this train through and throw toys to the children. Not good. Not new, either.

(Perhaps I ought to add here, before you start sending canned goods to people who live in million-dollar homes in West Virginia, that a good portion of Appalachia is not poor or needy or uneducated. And, gas prices being what they are, if you feel the need to be a do-gooder, you'll find plenty of poor people in the heart of the largest city close to you. Once you have made sure that all of those people have GED's, and jobs, and decent housing, and kids with vaccinations, then you can go and be a nuisance in Appalachia, but I assure you that by and large we are doing just as well as the rest of the country, thank you. For every kid who gets a present from the Santa Claus train there are a hundred who get the same presents your kids are getting. And, of course, quite a few who are getting ATV's, and ponies, and designer treehouses - same as everywhere. We have millionaires, too. You wouldn't know it from the stereotypes, though, would you?)

The last thing I want to talk about is art - the art of war. When I finished *The Ballad of Frankie Silver* and *The Songcatcher*, I addressed the issue of the Civil War in the mountains in my novel *Ghost Riders*. The mountain conflict was not the Civil War in the *Gone with the Wind* sense, but much more the Civil War in the sense of Afghanistan or Bosnia. It was a terrible, terrible time. Many of the mountain people stayed loyal to the Union, and thus they were persecuted, and, in one instance in western North Carolina, *massacred* for their loyalty to the U.S. (*Sodom Laurel, Madison County, North Carolina.*)

When I started looking into the methods and traditions of warfare, I discovered that the American Civil War was essentially Super Bowl 1863, and that we had been fighting that same damned war for more than 2000 years. Not only fighting the same war, but fighting it in the same sort of way and not learning a whole lot. In case you or anyone you know plans on going to West Point, please listen carefully.

In 225 BC, the Celts had moved into Western Europe. They started out as a people in Eastern Europe, and you can find the early Celtic artifacts and burial sites there. But by 225 BC they had moved west into France, and they had come to northern Italy in the Po Valley. The Romans did not like that. There had been border raids and the usual bad blood skirmishes between two cultures. Finally the Romans sent troops up there to confront the Celts. They lost a few of the battles, but finally the big one came at Telemon, in 225 BC in the Po Valley. The Celts did what they always do; they attacked. They had swords that were good for cutting, but not for thrusting. They let out enormous war cries (think *rebel yells*), and they charged. They wore very little, had no armor, and their shields were small. The Romans, however, had been fighting them for some years and had been taking note. Roman soldiers wore metal armor, carried sharp swords that thrust as well as cut, and they had shields as tall as they were. When the Celts came charging up to the enemy, they met a solid metal wall: the Romans had put all the shields together and stood behind them. Another problem for the Celts: their metal-working was less sophisticated than that of the Romans. When they cut or hacked with their swords, the weapons bent. To use the sword again, you'd have to unbend it. So, there you stood with your foot straightening out your sword. *Guess what happened next...*

The Celts lost 40,000 soldiers in that one battle, and 10,000 more were taken prisoner. That was pretty much the end of them as a threat to Rome.

They migrated west after that, into Britain. I could keep giving you accounts of cross-cultural skirmishes, but we can skip all the way to Culloden in 1746. From Marcy Moor outside the little town near Inverness, April 16, 1746, the Jacobites commanded by Charles Edward Stuart (aka, Bonnie Prince Charlie) meet the English commanded by the Duke of Cumberland. The Earl of Murray, quartermaster for the Prince's army, had left the rations back in Inverness. He brought the wrong size ammunition. Before the battle, the men

marched for 24 hours without having eaten. They were exhausted.
Their swords this time were huge claymores, hardly able to be lifted,
still no body armor... It's the Duke of Cumberland's birthday, literally
and figuratively. His men are well-armed. They have bayonets on the
end of their muskets. They have very effective cannons.

And what do the clans do? The same thing they did in 225 BC.
They all lined up in a straight line, and then they *charged* with heavy
sword towards the *bayonets*. The English rifle drill taught the soldier
not to bayonet the attacker coming straight on, but to aim at the one
to the side. If everyone works together, that's a killer. The man rushing
towards you has his arm raised with the sword, so if you go in from
the side, he's unprotected and you've got him. Two thousand soldiers
were killed that day on the Scots side. British losses: fifty men. And
that was the beginning of the conquest of Scotland, that led to the
Highland Clearances, and that whole chain of events that ended with
so many people coming to America.

I contend that if you want to understand the American Civil
War, forget *Gettysburg*. The film you really ought to watch is *Brave-
heart*, because there it is. Remember? 75% of the South: *Celtic*. Super
Bowl 1863: Gettysburg, Pennsylvania.

The other factor to remember is that Celts don't like trench
warfare. They don't like entrenchment, barricades, and breastworks.
They don't like hiding behind stuff. (I wish they would learn!) There's
no lack of courage or determination, but they honestly think that if
you charge and yell, you're strong and brave - that you can overcome
an enemy who is hiding behind fortifications. Gettysburg. Here are all
these men up on the hill with cannons and rifles, and the South tries
to take the hill. What they also did not realize was that much earlier in
the war, the rifles used by the Union - but not by the Confederacy -
had gained twice the range of the old weapons. So the boys in grey are

still fighting the Mexican War, the Battle of Culloden, Telemon, but the weaponry is advanced well beyond that. They are still trying to charge, but the enemy can shoot them from half a mile away. Out of 75,054 Confederate troops at Gettysburg, 22,634 were killed. Let me put that in perspective for you: they lost this number in just *two days* in Pennsylvania in 1863. We lost 55,000 in the whole Vietnam War, in more than ten years.

The Celtic soldier... Barry Sadler, who wrote the song "The Green Berets," also wrote a book called *The Universal Soldier*, a kind of science fiction/fantasy thing. In it, the hero was a kind of Roman Soldier. He can't die. He just keeps being a soldier in various armies all the way through history, and finally he gets to Vietnam. It's a *Sgt. Rock* sort of war book, but Sadler is on to something. If you watched the movie about Audie Murphy, the most highly decorated hero of World War II, you saw that in a way Audie Murphy *was* the Universal Soldier. I can see him, that same Steve McQueen body type, at Telemon, with his short sword and his inadequate shield. There he is at Culloden, trying to lift that big Claymore to charge against bayonets and cannons. There he is at Gettysburg in Pickett's charge – up against excellent, state-of-the-art rifles and fortifications. Audie Murphy, East Texas, yet 110% Celt.

Culture doesn't go away. In art, in music, in rural customs, and even in war, if you go back far enough, everything starts to make sense, and you begin to see the patterns, the family resemblances. Or as Pinero said: *"I believe the future is simply the past, entered through another gate."*

Magic Realism in Appalachia

Anne is driving alone down a dark forest road when she swerves to avoid a deer, sending her car into the ditch. Anne is unable to get the car out of the ditch, but she gets out to survey the damage.

If at this point a group of elves comes out of the forest and puts Anne's car back on the road for her, you know you are reading a fantasy narrative.

However, if Anne uses her cell phone to call AAA, and while she is waiting for the tow truck to arrive, some elves come out of the forest and stand around telling her what a bad driver she is - but they don't move the car and they leave before the tow truck arrives with no trace of their having been there - then the narrative you are reading is magic realism.

Magic realism - the blurring of the line between the real and the supernatural with the equal acceptance of both - is a concept that first appeared in art in the early twentieth century, and later became an important element in contemporary fiction.

Although people tend to associate literary magic realism primarily with Latin American writers who popularized the form (Gabriel Garcia Marquez, Isabel Allende), the blending of the fantastic with the everyday is easy to find in popular culture: In *Northern Exposure* when Ed the Inuit film buff spends a week hanging out with a spectral Shaman that no one else can see, or when the prophet Elijah visits Dr. Fleichman for Passover. Hardly an episode of the program goes by without some touch of the light fantastic. In *Sleepless in Seattle* when Tom Hanks' character sees his dead wife sitting at the other end of the sofa... or Rags the super-annuated dog on *Spin City* who occasionally croaks out (in Tim Allen's voice), "Please kill me."

Magic realism runs through Toni Morrison's *Beloved* and through the works of Salman Rushdie, Gunter Grass, and Derek Walcott.

Magic realism is certainly a component of Appalachian Ballad novels that I write. I use it not because it is a fashionable literary device, but because I found the elements of magic realism in the mountain culture, and I reported what I saw.

I can tell you the exact moment that I decided to incorporate the supernatural into my work.

In March of 1990 the first Ballad novel *If Ever I Return, Pretty Peggy-O* was published by Scribners. It seemed to be a strictly realistic novel about the effects of the past on a small Tennessee town – unless you happened to notice the character of Vernon Woolwine, which few people did. In the novel Vernon was described as a "Welfare-funded exercise in street theater." Vernon, unemployed and pleasantly daft, spent his days loitering around the courthouse square, dressed in a succession of costumes: Darth Vader, a cowboy, a pirate, and so on. He was quite real and everyone took him for granted. No one in the book – and very few readers, I might add – noticed that Vernon's costumes were the emotional barometer of the town. When he is dressed as a negative character, bad things happen in Hamelin; when he's a good guy, all goes well. In the Christmas eve scene in *The Hangman's Beautiful Daughter*, Vernon is nowhere to be seen, but he has left a snow-covered plaster garden gnome in his place on the park bench, while he... does what?

When *If Ever I Return, Pretty Peggy-O* was published in 1990 Scribners hosted a publication party for the book at that year's Appalachian Studies Conference at Unicoi State Park, near Helen, Georgia. The publisher sent my editor Susanne Kirk down from New

York to host the festivities. The magic realism probably began for Susanne when she was picked up at the Atlanta airport by Major Sue, an elfin army intelligence officer from Wisconsin, and driven up several hours north into the hills of Georgia to be set down in Helen, a Bavarian theme-park-style alpine village that has made many an unsuspecting traveler believe in magic realism – or at least in Oz.

The conference book party ended in the early afternoon, and that evening Susanne and I invited some of the conference attendees to a get-together in the cabin we had rented for the weekend at Unicoi State Park. The party consisted of eighteen professors, two bottles of wine, a bag full of whatever the convenience store had in the way of snacks, and Susanne, the major, and me. After an hour or so of pretzels and shop talk, the talk turned to the supernatural, and one by one we began to tell the family ghost story. These weren't "Give me back my golden arm" stories. Nothing Stephen King would buy you a cup of coffee for. They were little stories of supernatural happenings that occurred in the family. Nobody made much of them. They were just there. Most of them went something like this: "My grandmother was in the kitchen when she looked out the window over the sink and she saw my Uncle John walking across the yard. Now Uncle John lives in Cincinnati, so she wasn't expecting to see him, but she thought he might have driven in to surprise her. She hurried out into the yard, but she didn't see him. No car was in the drive way, and when she called out to Uncle John, there was no answer. Finally she gave up and as she was coming in the back door, the phone was ringing. It was the family in Cincinnati calling to say that Uncle John had died – just when she saw him in the yard."

It isn't an earth-shaking story, but when you hear more than a dozen similar stories at an academic party, it gives you pause.

We had Ph.D's in English and Appalachian Studies and mining engineering, people from Georgia and New York and everywhere in-between, and everyone there had a ghost story – everyone except Susanne and the two male professors.

The folklore scholar from Appalachian State wasn't surprised. "These stories tend to get passed down in the family by the women folk," she said. "Men don't hear about them." Wait until a multi-generational family holiday like Thanksgiving, she advised. After the meal is over, the men go out to watch television or talk among themselves, while the women congregate in the kitchen to do the dishes and put away the leftovers. Now, first the women tell childbirth horror stories. That will get any rookies out of the kitchen. After the uninitiated have fled, then they get down to it.

"I don't have any family ghost stories, either," said Susanne. "I grew up in Tucson."

The folklore professor looked at her for a long moment. "Ghosts don't have call-waiting."

But the rest of us had a swarm of tales: about a host of invisible beings who ford the Little Santeetlah River at twilight, speaking Cherokee and smelling of bear grease; about the girl who dropped a knife setting the table for a dumb supper and was stabbed by her husband years later... with the same knife; or the weary Confederate soldier who asks the re-enactors how to get back to his regiment.

"I left that thread out of the book," I said wistfully. "This streak of the supernatural runs deep through mountain families and I left it out. "

"You had to," said the folklore professor, who is Charlotte Ross, and who later became Nora Bonesteel. "*Peggy-O* is told from the male point of view. The element of magic didn't belong in the narrative."

"Maybe not," I said, "But it belongs in stories about Appalachia."

The next novel, *The Hangman's Beautiful Daughter* is the mirror opposite of the first novel. It is set in the winter, deals with the future, and is told from women's point of view. It also introduced the character of Nora Bonesteel, the mountain wise woman who knows things that will happen, who makes graveyard quilts, and talks to ghosts. In *She Walks These Hills*, Nora sees the ghost of the pioneer woman trying to get home since 1779, and in *The Rosewood Casket* she is haunted by her childhood friend, who never lived to grow up. In *The Songcatcher* (Dutton, May 2001) Nora tries to find an old ballad that the dead don't want remembered.

Through Nora Bonesteel I channel the Cherokee folk tales, the mountain legends, and the family ghost stories – changed, perhaps, to fit the narrative, but not invented, because I don't have to.

In Appalachia the magic is already here.

Nora Bonesteel and the Sight

Of all the characters I write about, Nora Bonesteel is the one that people seem most intrigued by. Nora appears again in my new Ballad novel *The Devil Amongst the Lawyers*, published in June 2010 by Thomas Dunne Books of New York. In the novel, Nora is a 13-year old girl just coming to terms with the Sight. We see her as a school girl, being scolded by her teacher for "making up things" about Cherokee villages, and trying to cope with the things she sees about troubled strangers. In *The Devil Amongst the Lawyers*, we learn a lot more about her family and her early life.

Nora Bonesteel is based on Charlotte Ross, a professor friend of mine at Appalachian State University. She is originally from north Georgia, and the Sight runs in her family. Nora's experiences in *The Hangman's Beautiful Daughter* are all based on real events in Charlotte's childhood. If you want to hear Nora Bonesteel's real family ghost stories, I persuaded Charlotte to make a cassette tape of some of her experiences, and it is available on my website: Charlotte Rosss: The Legend Lady

(http://www.sharynmccrumb.com/marketplace.asp)

Every so often readers ask me: Do I have The Sight ?

I do have the Sight only a little, tiny bit: flashes every so often, but nothing to brag about or to do anyone any good.

Here's an example of my "powers."

About ten years ago, my son's pet hamster Emma escaped from her cage. She had been gone for days, and although we had searched all over the place, we found no trace of her. Then one night I was up in my study at 2 a.m. writing. There was no noise in the house, nothing out of the ordinary. And suddenly I had a strong feeling that I ought to go in the kitchen and look in the sink cabinet in a tall glass pitcher we kept down there. There was absolutely no reason for me to do that, but I had an absolutely compelling urge to check there for the missing hamster.

Before I could think better of this impulse, I got up from my desk, walked to the kitchen, and opened the sink cabinet.

Sure enough, Emma the Hamster had somehow gotten into the closed sink cabinet, and she had slid down into the tall glass pitcher, from which she had been unable to get out. She must have been without food or water for two or three days by then, and she would have died had I not found her. I wasn't even surprised when I found her. I just knew she was there.

So, that's my psychic gift.

Some people stop plane crashes. I save hamsters.

I have no plans to start wearing a cape and spandex, but thanks for asking.

Reflections on Historical Fiction

1. Do you consider yourself to be as important and valid as an accredited historian?

I believe that historical novelists (if they are good, if they research well, and if they understand their subject matter) can be as valid and sometimes more important than an "accredited" historian. The difference between "truth" and "fiction" is often spurious. The Iliad is listed in fiction, but in the 1890's Heinrich Schliemann bought a shovel, went to the coast of Turkey, and found Troy. On the other hand, Mein Kampf is shelved under non-fiction.

One purpose of historical fiction is to make the reader feel the events of the time. I understood World War I by reading nonfiction accounts of that war, but it was not until I read the novel All Quiet on the Western Front that - in a visceral way - I got it. Erich Maria Remarque taught me more about the war than "accredited historians;" and Remarque lived through the fighting on the Western Front; most of the people who wrote the historical accounts did not. The fact that Remarque's book was a "novel" does not make it less accurate or less important.

I think my job as an historical novelist is to make people care - to feel the events, rather than just to know the facts in a clinical sense.

2. As a historical novelist, do you feel obligated to research as meticulously as a bona fide historian?

In the one case where an obscure mountain crime was the subject of a novel of mine and of several "non-fiction" books, *(The Ballad of Frankie Silver)* I found that I did *more* research than the non-fiction writers, and that I was more accurate in describing the events in the case.

I do exactly the same research that any historian would do, but then I have to go one step further and bring all that research to life, giving it emotional weight and sensory illumination. Historians draw a picture of a battle; historical novelists put you in it.

3. Should you research more, less, different than an historian?

Both more and in the final stage differently. Historians strive to be objective. I can take sides. Thus I have to know as much as I can to choose a side, and in creating a character I have to know how he'd think and feel and what other things in his era would influence his feelings – even to the point of knowing what songs might be in his head.

4. As a historical novelist, what can you do better than a historian to tell a historical account?

Since I don't have to be objective, I can make the reader experience the event through the eyes of one partisan character, and by doing so I can make the reader care deeply about the event.

I also try to experience what I can to find out what the physical sensations were. I have dressed in a Civil War uniform and fired a muzzle loader. I have sat in Tennessee's electric chair. I have done laps in a race car at Lowe's Motor Speedway. I visit every major place I write about.

I think there's more to history than reading papers in the archives.

5. Have you ever come closer to revealing an essential truth than historians who have written of the same events and subjects?

"Essential truths," hell. At times, I got the *facts* right, and they didn't.

In 1833, a mountain girl named Frankie Silver was hanged for murder in Morganton, NC. Two "historians" who wrote about the case interviewed some local residents in the 1990's and were told that Frankie Silver was hanged from a formal wooden trap-door style gallows. The locals said their grandparents remembered the event.

Elderly people in 1990 are claiming that their grandparents remembered an 1833 hanging? *I don't think so.*

A trap-door gallows in a small mountain town in 1833? *I don't think so.*

So I did some general research, using three other 19th century hangings for comparison.

1) **Nat Turner** - Virginia 1833

Although the sheriff wasn't sure they would have to hang Frankie Silver until the day of the execution (a pardon was expected), the Virginia authorities were quite sure they would hang Nat Turner.

They had weeks to prepare. Yet, by all accounts, those carrying out the execution simply strung him up from a tree, using a ladder to get him up to the high branch.

Would a county sheriff, who thought the hanging might not even take place, go to the trouble of building a gallows ? Would he even have the expertise to do it?

2) **Thomas P. Dula** - ("Tom Dooley") Statesville, NC, 1868 This execution took place only forty miles or so away from the site of Frankie Silver's hanging, and it happened 34 years later. Therefore, the execution technology should have been more advanced. A New York newspaper sent a reporter to cover that hanging, so we know how Tom Dula was hanged. And again - the county sheriff knew weeks in advance that Dula would be executed, so they had time to prepare. But according to eyewitness accounts, Tom Dula was stood on the back of a cart with a rope around his neck - no trapdoor! I found it hard to believe that a sheriff in a neighboring county, 34 years *earlier*, would have used a trapdoor gallows.

3) John Brown - Harpers Ferry, WV, 1859
In the execution of abolitionist John Brown, they did indeed use a formal gallows with a trap door, but there are two factors to be considered here: a) The authorities had weeks to prepare for the execution; b) It was not an execution carried out by a county sheriff. In this case, the Army Corps of Engineers with all its expertise and its budget, conducted the execution. If you have lots of money and trained engineers at your disposal, then you can have all the fancy frills you want at an event. But I contend that in the case of the hanging of Frankie Silver, neither the money nor the expertise was available.

The only pre-1870's executions in the U.S. that I could find using the trapdoor-gallows were those carried out by the government or the military. Small town county sheriffs, who might perform one execution a year, lacked the resources and the expertise to use such elaborate means.

So... in my novel I said that Frankie Silver was hanged from the back of a cart, and I still say that the non-fiction historians who said otherwise were wrong.

6. Do you feel you were acting as a historical revisionist?

No. I felt that I was using more common sense in interpreting the data. I have never knowingly been "revisionist" in dealing with historical events.

7. At any point in a historical novel, do you feel that you are taking liberties with the historical truth that a real historian wouldn't?

For example, in *Ghost Riders*, there is a scene in which I have North Carolina Governor Zebulon Vance reacting with rage to the report of the Sodom Laurel Massacre in his home county. I know he did react with rage to that news. Memoirs of that era and the governor's paper in the North Carolina Archives all say so. But since I don't know word-for-word exactly what he said when he heard the news, I was "inventing" words to show – dramatize – his response. A non-fiction historian would not do that. *I did not change the facts, though – I simply dramatized them.*

8 Where in your book does historical fact end and historical fiction begin?

Historical fiction begins when something cannot be verified, but I take my best guess based on thorough research. What kind of pie did Frankie Silver eat on the way to the gallows? I know she DID eat pie and that it was July in western North Carolina, so I'm guessing it was something like blackberry – too early for apple.

When a conversation took place in the pre-tape recorder-era and we have only the gist of it, I have to produce that conversation in dialogue, so I take my best guess – often after reading speeches made by the person in question, so that I can approximate their speech patterns.

Once for *Ghost Riders*, I took a fragment of something Zebulon Vance really said, and I elaborated on it to make it into a longer scene for my novel. I sent the finished scene to a Zebulon Vance scholar, who was unable to tell where the real Vance left off and my embellishment began. I felt that I had got it right.

9. What rules do you set for yourself in taking liberties with accepted historical truth?

Anything I can verify, I do verify. After that I do all the research I can to make the most-informed guess I can make. If you are writing a novel, you may have to tell what the historical figures are eating or wearing, and often that requires an educated guess.

10. Has the advent of the computer changed your methods of acquiring historical data, storing, verifying...

It has made the more obvious data more easily accessible. I could Google, say, the date of the Battle of Chickamauga, instead of having to look it up. But apart from the obvious, I do not trust on-line sources. What the internet has done is to make it easy to locate used, out-of-print reference books, and it enables me to order them via credit card from bookstores all over the world. That is a great savings of time and energy.

Further Comments

The Beagle story is a cautionary tale to demonstrate that historical research requires common sense, even if you're dealing with a primary source. Sometimes even they are wrong.

My friend Ward Burton is a race car driver who won the 2002 Daytona 500, but he is also known as a conservationist and wildlife advocate. Because he and I have been working on a memoir of his life, I have heard a great many tales of his boyhood adventures. This is Ward Burton's Beagle story.

As Ward tells it, when he was six years old, his father told him that he could have a puppy. Being a huntin' family from a small town in rural Virginia, hunting for a young boy meant running rabbits and taking potshots at squirrels; of course, his new puppy would be a beagle.

So to hear Ward tell it, "One Saturday morning my dad took me to a farm where the man had a beagle with a litter of ten pups. And I went to the pen and I looked at all those pups, and I said, 'Nope. My dog's not here.' And we left."

"You left?" I said.

"Yeah."

"Without a puppy?"

"Yeah."

"And you were six years old ?"

"Yeah."

"Then what?"

"The next week he took me to another place with a litter of beagle pups. And I looked 'em all over, and I said again, 'My dog's not here.' And Dad took me home." He beams with pride at how he had maintained his high standards. "We must'a gone to four or five places before I finally found the right dog," he says.

"And... you... were... six...years...old ?"

"Yep."

"And you weren't into show dogs, or breeding stock, or anything?"

"Naw. Just wanted a pet. Teach him to hunt rabbits in the woods, with my .22."

"That story doesn't make any damn sense. No six-year old behaves like that."

"Well, I did."

"WHY?"

"'Cause I'm just particular."

A year after I heard that tale, I still thought a big piece of the puzzle was missing. I was visiting him in his home town one day, and we met his father. With Ward still in the room, I decided to ask his father about the beagle story. I said to him, "Tell me about Ward's first dog."

"Rebel the First, you mean? We named all our beagles Rebel."

"Tell me how you got him."

"Well," said his dad. "I was driving down the road one day, and I saw a Beagle puppy by the side of the road with his head stuck in a mayonnaise jar. (It was trying to lick the last dregs of mayonnaise out of the jar and got caught.) So I stopped to help it. I had to break the jar with a rock, and then I took the pup home and had to file the jar rim off of his neck. So we kept him."

Ward is now muttering, "I forgot about that!"

I gave him a "you-shut-up" look. And then I said to his father, "So you kept that beagle puppy. *And did that dog die when Ward was six years old?*"

"Why, yes," said his dad. "How did you know?"

Because it was the only thing that made sense. My boy is not a discerning judge of canine excellence, he is just an anal-retentive little control freak who *never wants anything to change.*

Not even the markings on a dog.

He kept turning down puppies until he found one whose markings matched the dog who had just died. But over the years, Ward forgot *why* he had turned down all those puppies. He forgot the original dog. But he remembered the quest. *Now* it made sense.

Isn't that a great story? I use it when I teach writers workshops on research. I tell writers that if they come across a true anecdote that does not make sense, it means they are missing a key piece of the puzzle, and they have to keep digging until they find it.

That really impressed Ward at the time. He thought it was magic that I knew there was part of the story missing.

But one of my strongest beliefs is *that if you have enough information, everything will make sense.* If it doesn't make sense, you need to keep digging.

This is exactly the logic I used when I considered the case of the 1866 murder of Laura *Foster in my novel The Ballad of Tom Dooley.* The story did not make sense as people traditionally told it.

When I worked on an article about Tom Dooley for *Blue Ridge Country Magazine*, my travel companion and I went through all the possibilities inherent in the love triangle. None of them worked.

Tom killed Laura Foster because she gave him syphilis.

There is no evidence that she did. Patient Zero was Pauline Foster, with whom Tom had sexual relations. It is more likely that he gave the disease to Laura instead of vice-versa.

Tom killed Laura Foster because she was pregnant.

There is no evidence that she was. Dr. Carter did not note the presence of fetal bones in the autopsy. Besides, Laura had a reputation for promiscuity. Judging by the example of Ann's mother, who had five children and no husband, pregnancy in that place and time would not have made marriage compulsory. If Tom had dallied with a planter's daughter or a lawyer's sister - sure. But not with an unchaste tenant farmer's daughter.

Ann Foster Melton killed Laura Foster because Tom loved her and was planning to elope with her.

Tom said more than once that he "had no use for Laura Foster," and I believe him. If Ann had killed the woman he truly loved, would he have written a confession exonerating Ann on the eve of his execution?

Tom and Ann killed Laura Foster. Motive unspecified.

Why? She had no money, no hold over them, and apparently no malice toward them.

James Melton or Pauline Foster killed Laura Foster.
Neither was ever suspected of involvement in the death of Laura Foster, and neither of them had the slightest motive to dispense with her. Besides, if either of them had done it, Tom Dula and Ann Melton would certainly have saved themselves by denouncing the real killer. They did not.

I concluded that there was a missing piece of the puzzle, because one could not construct a plausible scenario with the traditional collection of facts.

When I read the trial transcripts and the newspaper coverage of Dula's execution, I found three references to a fourth person in this supposed "love triangle," a detail roundly ignored in other studies of the case – but he was real, and he was there. He was "the missing beagle" in the scenario. That story of a young boy and a dog is of no consequence in historical terms but as an exercise in analytical thought, it is priceless.

About the Author

Sharyn McCrumb is an award-winning Southern writer, best known for her Appalachian "Ballad" novels, set in the North Carolina/Tennessee mountains, including the New York Times Best Sellers *She Walks These Hills*, *The Rosewood Casket*, and *The Ballad of Frankie Silver*.

Her most recent novel is a new Ballad novel, *The Devil Amongst the Lawyers* (Thomas Dunne Books, June 2010), which was a finalist for the Weatherford Award for Appalachian fiction, and is a nominee for SIBA Book of the Year. Coming in August 2011, *The Ballad of Tom Dooley*, also from Thomas Dunne Books/St. Martins Press, New York, tells the true story behind the folk song.

St. Dale, The Canterbury Tales in a NASCAR setting, in which ordinary people on a pilgrimage in honor of racing legend Dale Earnhardt find a miracle, won a 2006 Library of Virginia Award as well as the AWA Book of the Year Award.

McCrumb, who has been named a "Virginia Woman of History" in 2008 for Achievement in Literature, was a guest author at the National Festival of the Book in Washington, D.C. sponsored by the White House in 2006.

Sharyn McCrumb's other best-selling novels include *The Ballad of Frankie Silver*, the story of the first woman hanged for murder in the state of North Carolina; and *The Songcatcher*, a genealogy in music, tracing the author's family from 18th century Scotland to the present by following a Scots Ballad through the generations. *Ghost Riders*, an account of the Civil War in the mountains of western North Carolina, won the *Wilma Dykeman Award* for Literature given by the East Tennessee Historical Society and the *Audie Award* for Best Recorded Book.

McCrumb's other honors include: AWA Outstanding Contribution to Appalachian Literature Award; the Chaffin Award for Southern Literature; the Plattner Award for Short Story; and AWA's Best Appalachian Novel. A graduate of UNC- Chapel Hill, with an M.A. in English from Virginia Tech, McCrumb was the first writer-in-residence at King College in Tennessee. In 2005 she honored as the Writer of the Year at Emory & Henry College.

Her novels, studied in universities throughout the world, have been translated into eleven languages, including French, German, Dutch, Japanese, Arabic, and Italian. She has lectured on her work at Oxford University, the University of Bonn-Germany, and at the Smithsonian Institution; taught a writers workshop in Paris, and served as writer-in-residence at King College in Tennessee and at the Chautauqua Institute in western New York. She is the subject of the book From A Race of Storytellers: The Ballad Novels of Sharyn McCrumb. Ed: Kimberley M. Holloway. Atlanta: Mercer University Press, 2005.

A film of the novel *The Rosewood Casket* is currently in development, directed by British Academy Award nominee Roberto Schaefer.

Sharyn McCrumb is a graduate of UNC Chapel Hill, with an M.A. from Virginia Tech. She lives and writes near Roanoke, Virginia.

CPSIA information can be obtained at www.ICGtesting.com
Printed in the USA
242359LV00003B/75/P